WALTZ
WITH
BASHIR

WALTZ WITH BASHIR

A LEBANON WAR STORY

ARI FOLMAN
DAVID POLONSKY

Metropolitan Books
Henry Holt and Company • New York

Metropolitan Books
Henry Holt and Company, LLC
Publishers since 1866
175 Fifth Avenue
New York, New York 10010
www.henryholt.com

Metropolitan Books® and ® are registered trademarks of Henry Holt and Company, LLC.

Library of Congress Cataloging-in-Publication Data

Folman, Ari.
   Waltz with Bashir : a Lebanon war story / Ari Folman, David Polonsky — 1st U.S. ed.
      p. cm.
   ISBN-13: 978-0-8050-8673-7 (hardcover)
   ISBN-10: 0-8050-8673-0 (hardcover)
   ISBN-13: 978-0-8050-8892-2 (pbk.)
   ISBN-10: 0-8050-8892-X (pbk.)
 1. Folman, Ari—Comic books, strips, etc. 2. Soldiers—Israel—Biography—Comic books, strips, etc. 3.
Sabra and Shatila Massacre, Lebanon, 1982—Personal narratives, Israeli—Comic books, strips, etc. 4.
Lebanon—History—Israeli intervention, 1982–1984—Atrocities—Comic books, strips, etc. 5. Graphic
novels. I. Polonsky, David. II. Title.
DS87.53.F65 2008
956.9204'4—dc22   2008023322

Henry Holt books are available for special promotions and premiums.
For details contact: Director, Special Markets.

First U.S. Edition 2009
Printed in China
10 9 8 7 6 5 4 3 2 1

WALTZ
WITH
BASHIR

THE NIGHT BOAZ CALLED WAS THE WORST NIGHT THAT WINTER.
IT WAS JANUARY 2006. NOTHING IN OUR THIRTY YEARS OF FRIENDSHIP
HAD PREPARED ME FOR THE STORY HE WAS ABOUT TO TELL.

THE DOGS HAVE BEEN COMING FOR TWO YEARS, HE SAID.

3

TWENTY-SIX DOGS.

I SEE THEIR MEAN FACES FROM THE WINDOW. THEY'VE COME TO KILL ME.

THEY TELL BERTOLD, THE GUY WHO OWNS THE OFFICE DOWNSTAIRS, EITHER GIVE US BOAZ REIN'S HEAD OR WE'LL EAT YOUR CLIENTS. YOU'VE GOT ONE MINUTE.

AT THE BEGINNING OF THE WAR, IN THE SUMMER OF '82, WE'D GO INTO THE VILLAGES SEARCHING FOR PALESTINIANS ON OUR WANTED LIST.

WHEN YOU COME TO A VILLAGE THE DOGS SMELL YOU FIRST AND START BARKING.

THE WHOLE VILLAGE WAKES UP AND THE MAN YOU'RE LOOKING FOR GETS AWAY.

SOMEONE HAD TO FINISH THE DOGS OFF. THEY KNEW I WAS INCAPABLE OF SHOOTING PEOPLE, SO THEY SAID, OKAY BOAZ...

THAT NIGHT...

...FOR THE FIRST TIME IN TWENTY YEARS...

...I HAD A TERRIBLE FLASHBACK FROM THE LEBANON WAR.

...BUT FROM THE NIGHT OF THE MASSACRE...

...IN THE SABRA AND SHATILA REFUGEE CAMPS.

14

MEMORY IS A VERY INTERESTING THING. I'LL TELL YOU ABOUT A WELL-KNOWN EXPERIMENT IN PSYCHOLOGY.

THEY SHOWED A GROUP OF PEOPLE PICTURES FROM THEIR CHILDHOOD. MOST PICTURES WERE OF THINGS THAT HAD REALLY HAPPENED.

ONE PICTURE, OF AN AMUSEMENT PARK, WAS PHONY.

THEY PLANTED IMAGES OF THE CHILDREN IN A PHOTO OF THE PARK, WHICH THEY HAD NEVER ACTUALLY VISITED.

EIGHTY PERCENT OF THE PEOPLE SAW THEMSELVES IN THE PHONY PICTURE AND REMEMBERED THE EVENT, EVEN THOUGH IT HAD NEVER HAPPENED.

THE RESEARCHERS TOLD THE OTHER TWENTY PERCENT...

...TO "GO HOME AND THINK ABOUT IT."

WHEN THEY SAW THE PICTURE AGAIN, EACH ONE SAID...

..."YES, I REMEMBER BEING AT THE AMUSEMENT PARK WITH MY PARENTS AND HAVING A WONDERFUL DAY."

CARMI'S BEEN LIVING IN HOLLAND FOR THE PAST TWENTY YEARS. I'D ALWAYS WANTED TO VISIT HIM BUT SOMEHOW IT NEVER HAPPENED. IT WAS KIND OF WEIRD TO GO THERE AFTER ALL THIS TIME ON THE PRETEXT OF RESEARCHING A FORGOTTEN WAR.

SEE ALL THIS?

IT'S ALL MINE.

FROM THOSE TREES OVER THERE TO THE RIVER ON THE OTHER SIDE. ABOUT TEN ACRES.

ALL THIS FROM SELLING FALAFEL?

YEAH, ALL THIS FROM SELLING FALAFEL.

I THOUGHT I WAS THE ONLY ONE WITH MASCULINITY PROBLEMS. SO I HAD TO PROVE THAT I WAS A GREAT FIGHTER, A BIG HERO.

BUT THEN THE WAR STARTED AND THEY PUT US ON THIS FUCKING LOVE BOAT.

AND ME...

...I BEGAN PUKING LIKE A PIG,

WORRYING ABOUT WHAT THE ENEMY WOULD THINK IF THEY SAW ME LIKE THIS.

THEN I COLLAPSED ON THE DECK AND FELL ASLEEP.

I ALWAYS FALL ASLEEP WHEN I'M SCARED.

...AND I GET LAID FOR THE FIRST TIME.

FROM A DISTANCE, I SEE MY FRIENDS...

...GOING UP IN FLAMES...

...RIGHT BEFORE MY EYES.

I WAKE UP JUST BEFORE WE LAND.

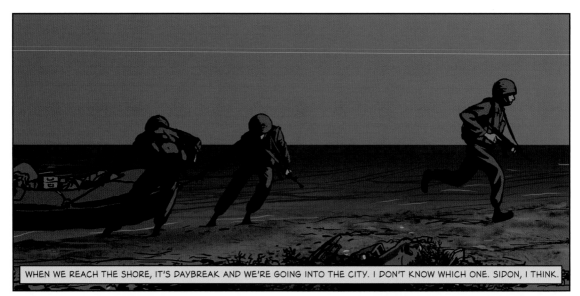

WHEN WE REACH THE SHORE, IT'S DAYBREAK AND WE'RE GOING INTO THE CITY. I DON'T KNOW WHICH ONE. SIDON, I THINK.

WITH ALL THE PRESSURE AND THE FEAR, WE START SHOOTING LIKE MANIACS. I HAVE NO IDEA AT WHAT.

I SEE A BLUE MERCEDES COMING DOWN THE ROAD AND EVERYONE'S FIRING AT IT LIKE CRAZY.

EVEN AFTER TWO YEARS OF TRAINING, THERE'S NOTHING BUT UNCONTROLLABLE FEAR. AND THEN SILENCE, THE HORRIFIC SILENCE OF DEATH.

WHEN IT'S FULLY LIGHT, YOU SEE THE HAVOC YOU'VE CAUSED.

AND LYING IN THE CAR...

...ARE THE BODIES OF A FAMILY.

IN THE EVENING WE STOP. AN OFFICER COMES OVER TO US.

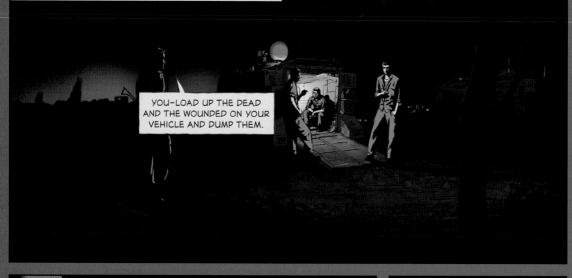

YOU—LOAD UP THE DEAD AND THE WOUNDED ON YOUR VEHICLE AND DUMP THEM.

DUMP THEM?

YEAH, DUMP THEM.

DUMP THEM WHERE?

HOW SHOULD I KNOW? LOOK FOR A BRIGHT LIGHT. THAT'S WHERE THEY USUALLY DUMP THE BODIES.

SO I FIND MYSELF GOING BACK THE WAY WE CAME. ME, WHO IN MY WHOLE LIFE HAS HARDLY SEEN A DROP OF BLOOD, LET ALONE AN OPEN WOUND, SUDDENLY I'M COMMANDING AN APC FULL OF INJURED SOLDIERS AND DEAD MEN, LOOKING FOR A BRIGHT LIGHT.

WHAT ARE WE SUPPOSED TO BE DOING? WHY DON'T YOU TELL US WHAT TO DO?

SHOOT.

AT WHAT?

I DON'T KNOW. JUST SHOOT.

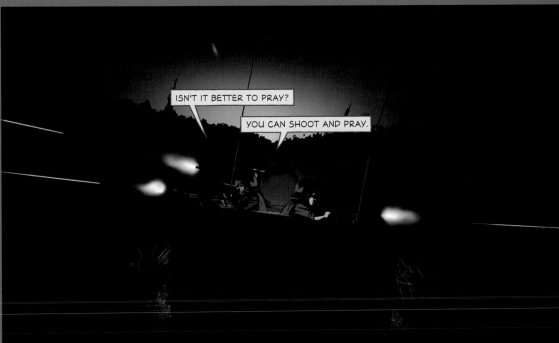

ISN'T IT BETTER TO PRAY?

YOU CAN SHOOT AND PRAY.

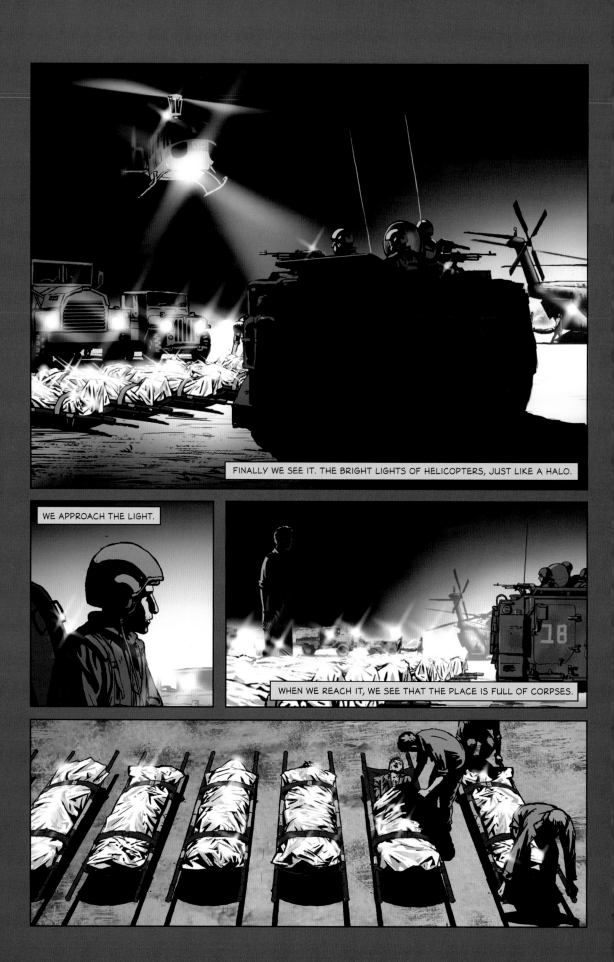

FINALLY WE SEE IT. THE BRIGHT LIGHTS OF HELICOPTERS, JUST LIKE A HALO.

WE APPROACH THE LIGHT.

WHEN WE REACH IT, WE SEE THAT THE PLACE IS FULL OF CORPSES.

MY NEXT STEP WAS TO FIND SOMEONE WHO WAS THERE THAT FIRST NIGHT OF THE WAR, MAYBE EVEN SOMEONE I'D BROUGHT TO THE PLACE WITH THE BRIGHT LIGHT. IT TOOK A WHILE, BUT THE SEARCH LED TO RONNIE DAYAG, A BIOLOGIST.

IS IT POSSIBLE THAT I EVACUATED SOME OF YOUR GUYS?

MAYBE. WE WERE IN THE COASTAL AREA IN THE WESTERN SECTOR. YES. IT SOUNDS LOGICAL.

DO YOU RECOGNIZE ME HERE?

NO, NO.

I DON'T RECOGNIZE MYSELF EITHER.

WE CROSSED THE BORDER AT ROSH HANIKRA. IT FELT LIKE WE WERE GOING ON A TRIP.

WE TOOK PICTURES, TOLD JOKES. WE HAD SOME TIME TO FOOL AROUND.

34

THE LANDSCAPE WAS BEAUTIFUL, TREES EVERYWHERE, A FEW HOUSES HERE AND THERE, REALLY PASTORAL.

WE DROVE SLOWLY. I WAS WITH MY COMMANDER, ENJOYING THE SCENERY.

THE ONLY THOUGHT IN MY HEAD WAS, THAT'S THE END, FOR ME IT'S OVER.

I COULD SEE OUR COMPANY COMMANDER'S TANK. I HOPED SOMEHOW HE'D COME CLOSER. BUT INSTEAD HE STARTED RETREATING. I WAS ALONE.

THERE WAS NOTHING TO DO BUT WAIT FOR THE END.

I THOUGHT ABOUT MY MOTHER AND HOW SHE WOULD REACT. SHE'S VERY ATTACHED TO ME. I'VE ALWAYS BEEN HER RIGHT HAND. I'M THE ONE WHO HELPS OUT AT HOME.

THEN I TOOK A PEEK. I COULD SEE THE PALESTINIANS TALKING, LAUGHING, SMOKING. I WAS SURPRISED THEY WEREN'T LOOKING IN MY DIRECTION. AFTER A WHILE I REALIZED THAT THEY PROBABLY THOUGHT WE'D ALL BEEN KILLED IN THE ATTACK.

I THOUGHT I'D WAIT UNTIL DARK. IT WAS A PRETTY GOOD PLACE TO HIDE.

I DON'T KNOW WHY, BUT WHEN THE EVENING CAME, I DECIDED TO CRAWL TO THE SEA.

I DIDN'T WANT TO STAY TOO CLOSE TO THE SHORE, SO I SWAM OUT TO WHERE IT WAS DEEPER.

WHEN I THOUGHT I'D GONE FAR ENOUGH, I TURNED SOUTH, TOWARD HOME.

THE WATER WAS VERY QUIET, CALM, THERE WERE
HARDLY ANY WAVES. IT WAS JUST ME AND THE SEA.

I FELT A KIND OF PEACE BECAUSE
THE SEA WAS SO CALM, LIKE IT WAS
ON MY SIDE.

BUT AT THE SAME TIME I WAS
TERRIFIED THAT SOMEBODY WOULD
SEE ME AND SHOOT ME AND KILL ME.
I KEPT SWIMMING IN THE STILLNESS, BUT
THEN I BEGAN LOSING MY STRENGTH.
I COULDN'T MOVE MY LIMBS.

THERE WERE MOMENTS WHERE I JUST
FLOATED AND LET THE WATER CARRY ME.

SOMEHOW I REACHED THE SHORE. I'D SEEN LIGHTS IN THE DISTANCE AND DECIDED THAT WAS MY GOAL. MAYBE THEY WERE ISRAELI FORCES.

SUDDENLY I HEARD VOICES COMING OVER A RADIO, SPEAKING HEBREW.

I HAD TO GET THERE. I MOVED VERY SLOWLY. THE VOICES GREW LOUDER.

TO MY AMAZEMENT, I'D RUN RIGHT INTO THE REGIMENT THAT HAD ABANDONED ME. LATER THEY TOLD ME THAT I'D SWUM FIVE MILES.

AFTER I REJOINED THEM, I FELT AS IF I'D SOMEHOW ABANDONED THEM. I HAD THE FEELING THEY SAW ME AS SOMEONE WHO'D DESERTED HIS FRIENDS, WHO'D RUN FROM THE BATTLEFIELD TO SAVE HIS OWN SKIN.

I CUT MYSELF OFF FROM MY FRIENDS' FAMILIES. AT FIRST I VISITED THEIR GRAVES, BUT I DIDN'T WANT TO BE THERE. I WANTED TO FORGET.

WHEN YOU GO TO THE CEMETERY, YOU FEEL...GUILTY.

IT'S AS IF I DIDN'T DO ENOUGH. I WASN'T THE KIND OF HERO WHO PULLS OUT HIS WEAPONS AND SAVES EVERYONE.

THAT'S NOT WHO I AM.

A MONTH AFTER RONNIE DAYAG HAD SWUM BACK TO HIS REGIMENT...

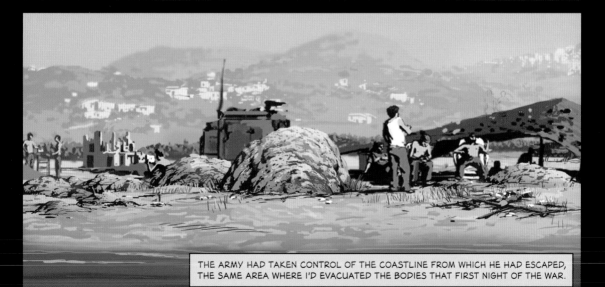

THE ARMY HAD TAKEN CONTROL OF THE COASTLINE FROM WHICH HE HAD ESCAPED,
THE SAME AREA WHERE I'D EVACUATED THE BODIES THAT FIRST NIGHT OF THE WAR.

THEY KEPT TELLING US THAT SOON WE'D INVADE BEIRUT AND WE WERE GOING TO DIE.

BUT WE WERE ALL HANGING OUT, DOWN ON THE BEACH.

AND WE WEREN'T THINKING MUCH ABOUT DEATH.

THESE DAYS, FRENKEL IS THE NATIONAL CHAMPION IN DENNIS SURVIVAL JU JITSU, A LOCAL MARTIAL ART THAT COMBINES KARATE, JUDO, AND FREE-STYLE STREET FIGHTING. IT'S A POSITION HE'S HELD FOR THE LAST EIGHT YEARS.

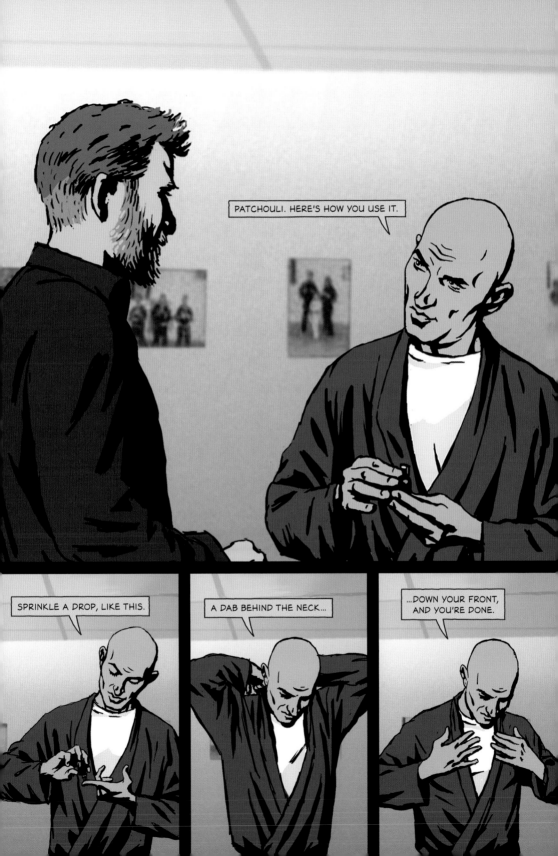

SO, THE DAILY ROUTINE BACK THEN: WE'D GET UP IN THE MORNING.

WE FIXED OUR BREAKFAST RIGHT THERE ON THE BEACH, CANNED BEEF AND EGGS.

THE ORDER WOULD COME DOWN:

SEND OUT THE MEN.

GET YOUR GEAR...

...PUT ON YOUR FLAK JACKETS...

...AND GO HUNT FOR TERRORISTS.

WE WERE DOWN ON THE GROUND.

I HEARD SOMEONE YELL, "FRENKEL!"

THROUGH THE TREES I SAW A BOY STANDING THERE, A BOY WITH AN RPG.

UNTIL SOMETHING HAPPENED AND IT WAS AS IF HIS CAMERA HAD BROKEN.

HE SAID, "LOOK, IT WAS A REALLY TERRIBLE MOMENT. WE GOT TO THE HIPPODROME IN BEIRUT, WHERE THE STABLES WERE...

...AND I SAW ALL THESE BODIES, THESE CORPSES OF BEAUTIFUL ARABIAN HORSES. THEY'D BEEN SLAUGHTERED. IT BROKE MY HEART."

"WAR IS BAD ENOUGH, THE THINGS PEOPLE DO TO EACH OTHER", HE TOLD ME, "BUT WHAT HAD THESE LOVELY HORSES DONE, WHAT SIN HAD THEY COMMITTED, THAT THEY HAD TO SUFFER THIS WAY?"

THE PILE OF HORSES WAS TOO MUCH FOR HIM TO BEAR. THE MECHANISM HE'D USED TO PROTECT HIMSELF, TO KEEP HIM OUT OF THE FRAME, AS IF HE WERE WATCHING A FILM BUT NOT PARTICIPATING IN IT, FAILED HIM.

HE HAD BEEN PULLED INTO THE PICTURE, AND THEN HE LOST HIS MIND.

YOU SAID YOU DON'T REMEMBER BEING IN THE ORCHARD WITH THE RPG KID. DO YOU REMEMBER OTHER THINGS FROM THAT PERIOD?

YES, I REMEMBER MY HOME LEAVE IN DETAIL.

WHEN I CAME HOME FROM LEBANON FOR THE FIRST TIME IN SIX WEEKS, LIFE WAS GOING ON AS NORMAL.

I THOUGHT ABOUT HOW WHEN I WAS A KID, THERE WAS A WAR GOING ON....

...AND EVERYTHING HAD COME TO A HALT.

THE FATHERS WERE ALL AWAY ON THE FRONT LINE.

SHE'D BROKEN UP WITH ME JUST BEFORE THE WHOLE THING HAD STARTED.

ANYWAY, I WAS SENT TO THIS VILLA ON THE OUTSKIRTS OF BEIRUT.

THE PLACE WAS FULL OF GOLD, MARBLE, GOLD FAUCETS, YOU NAME IT.

SO WE WAITED ALL NIGHT, WATCHING FOR THE MERCEDES...

...EXPECTING SOME DREADFUL DISASTER.

AND THEN, JUST BEFORE DAWN, THE PHONE RANG.

BASHIR'S DEAD.

BASHIR WHO?

BASHIR JUMAYEL, PRESIDENT OF LEBANON. A BROTHER, AN ALLY, A CHRISTIAN. ONE OF US. MURDERED.

"GET EVERYONE UP," HE SAID. "YOU'RE IN BEIRUT IN TWO HOURS."

AT SOME POINT I BROKE AWAY AND WENT UP TO THE TERMINAL.

I FOUND MYSELF ON A KIND OF TRIP, LIKE I WAS HALLUCINATING...

...AS THOUGH I REALLY WAS IN AN INTERNATIONAL AIRPORT.

ALL I HAD TO DO WAS CHOOSE, DECIDE ON A DESTINATION.

I STOOD IN FRONT OF THE DEPARTURES BOARD AND SAID TO MYSELF, OKAY, JUST CHOOSE.

I COULD TAKE THE 14:10 TO LONDON, THE 15:20 TO PARIS, THE 16:00 TO NEW YORK.

I CARRIED ON WANDERING AROUND THE TERMINAL...

...LOOKING AT THE DUTY FREE SHOPS, THE JEWELRY, TOBACCO, ALCOHOL.

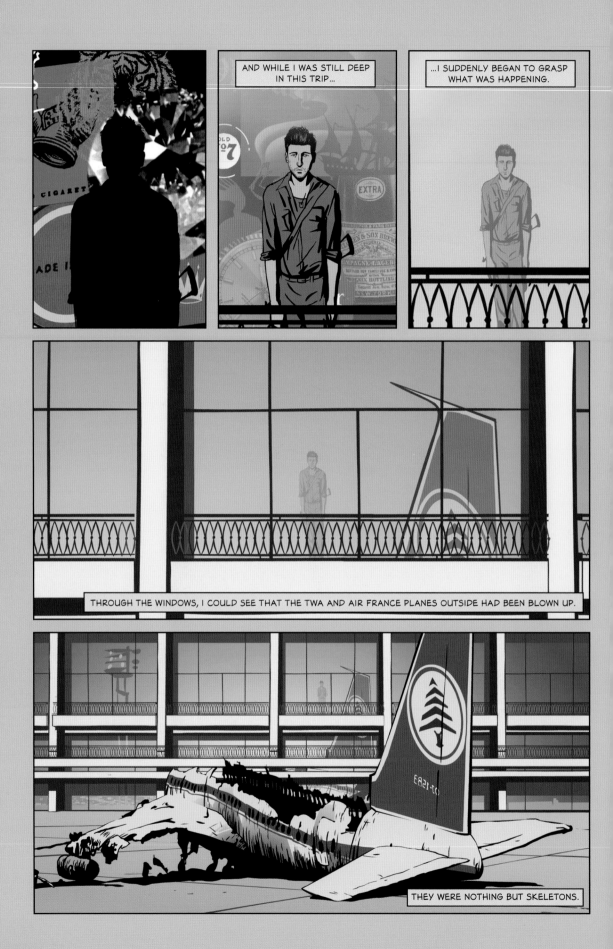

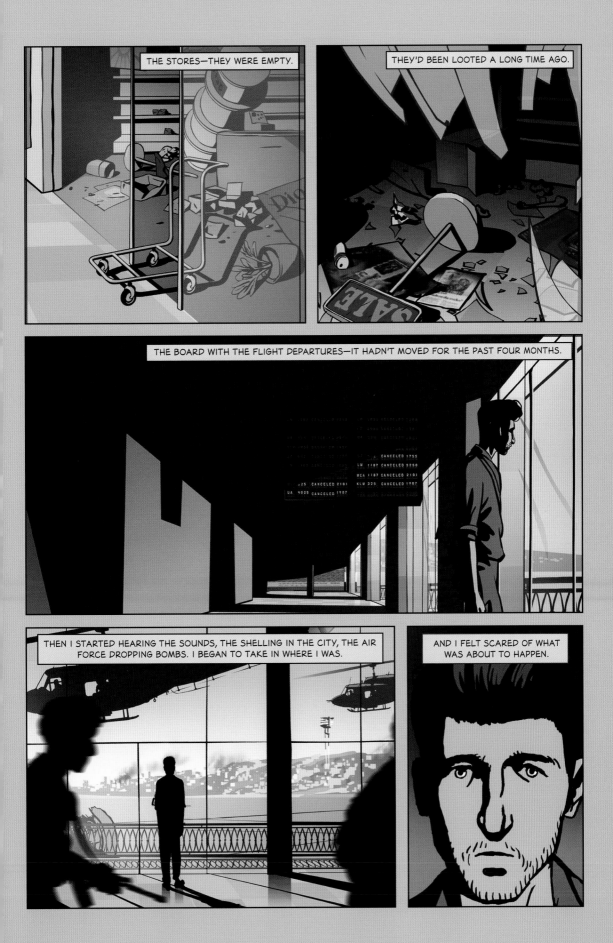

THE STORES—THEY WERE EMPTY.

THEY'D BEEN LOOTED A LONG TIME AGO.

THE BOARD WITH THE FLIGHT DEPARTURES—IT HADN'T MOVED FOR THE PAST FOUR MONTHS.

THEN I STARTED HEARING THE SOUNDS, THE SHELLING IN THE CITY, THE AIR FORCE DROPPING BOMBS. I BEGAN TO TAKE IN WHERE I WAS.

AND I FELT SCARED OF WHAT WAS ABOUT TO HAPPEN.

WE STARTED WALKING INTO THE CITY.

TOWERING ABOVE US WERE MASSIVE MULTI-STORY HOTELS.

TO THE SIDE OF US WAS THE SEA.

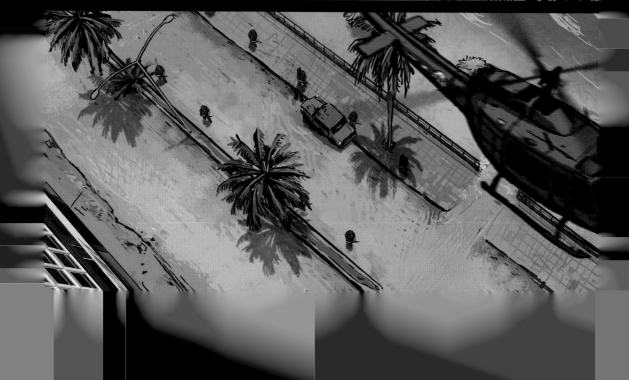

WE WERE WALKING ALONG A KIND OF PROMENADE GOING TOWARD A BIG INTERSECTION. WE HAD NO WAY OF TELLING WHO WAS A SNIPER...

...AND WHO WAS A MUSICIAN.

THEN, SUDDENLY, THE SNIPERS STARTED, FIRING DOWN ON US FROM THE HOTELS.

WE COULDN'T SEE WHERE THE FIRE WAS COMING FROM, WHO WAS SHOOTING, WHAT THEY WERE SHOOTING, NOTHING.

THERE WAS A SOLDIER WOUNDED, LYING IN THE MIDDLE OF THE INTERSECTION. BUT THERE WAS NO WAY TO GET TO HIM.

WE WERE SO SCARED.

WE WERE SCARED OUT OF OUR MINDS.

AND IN THE MIDDLE OF THIS TOTAL HELL, THAT JOURNALIST FROM THE TV SHOWED UP, RON BEN-YISHAI.

HE WAS STRIDING THROUGH THE BULLETS, TALL, UPRIGHT, SUPERMAN, WALKING AS IF THERE WAS NOTHING GOING ON.

THE BULLETS WERE DOING ZIG-ZAGS OVER HIS HEAD, AND JUST IN FRONT OF HIM THERE WAS A CAMERAMAN, SHAKING WITH FEAR, CRAWLING ON ALL FOURS, BLINDED BY HIS HELMET.

RON BEN-YISHAI, ISRAEL'S GREATEST WAR CORRESPONDENT, HADN'T FORGOTTEN THE MADNESS THAT DAY ON HAMRA STREET.

THERE WAS A TREMENDOUS HISSING SOUND. THEY WERE FIRING MASSES OF RPGS, LIKE IN A SHOOTING RANGE. BEFORE THEY EXPLODE, AS THEY COME OVER, THE RPGS MAKE THIS WHIZZING NOISE, AND THERE'S THE PING OF THE SHELLS RICOCHETING OFF THE WALLS.

AND WITH ALL THIS GOING ON, THERE WERE CIVILIANS, STANDING OUT ON THEIR BALCONIES—WOMEN, CHILDREN, OLD PEOPLE, WATCHING AS IF THEY WERE AT A MOVIE.

FROM WHERE I WAS CROUCHING, I WATCHED FRENKEL TAKE THE INTERSECTION.

I DON'T KNOW WHETHER IT LASTED FOR ETERNITY OR FOR A MINUTE...

...BUT HE STAYED IN THE STREET, WITH BULLETS RAINING DOWN ON HIM...

...AND BEGAN TO DANCE.

THE SNIPERS WERE NOTHING TO HIM, HE WAS IN A TRANCE. HE DANCED AS IF HE MEANT TO STAY THERE FOREVER...

IT WAS A JUNKYARD WHERE THEY TOOK THE PALESTINIANS TO INTERROGATE THEM. THEN THEY MURDERED THEM.

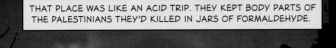

THAT PLACE WAS LIKE AN ACID TRIP. THEY KEPT BODY PARTS OF THE PALESTINIANS THEY'D KILLED IN JARS OF FORMALDEHYDE.

YOU COULD SEE FINGERS INSIDE A JAR, EYES, YOU NAME IT.

THE PHALANGISTS ALWAYS HAD PICTURES OF BASHIR ON THEM. BASHIR PENDANTS, BASHIR WATCHES, BASHIR THIS, BASHIR THAT.

THE MAN WAS THEIR IDOL, THEIR SUPERSTAR.

WHAT THEY FELT FOR HIM WAS EROTIC.

AND JUST BEFORE THEIR IDOL IS ABOUT TO BE CROWNED KING, HE'S MURDERED.

IT WAS OBVIOUS THEY'D AVENGE HIS DEATH IN A TOTALLY SICK WAY.

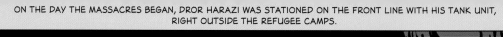

ON THE DAY THE MASSACRES BEGAN, DROR HARAZI WAS STATIONED ON THE FRONT LINE WITH HIS TANK UNIT, RIGHT OUTSIDE THE REFUGEE CAMPS.

THEY SENT US TO A CERTAIN POST. IT WAS MORE LIKE A HILL, OVERLOOKING THE WESTERN PART OF THE CAMPS.

FROM MY POSITION I COULD SEE A RESIDENTIAL AREA, HOUSES.

EVERY NOW AND THEN THE PALESTINIANS FIRED AT US. WE'D TRY TO LOCATE THE SOURCE OF THE FIRE AND RETALIATE.

MEANWHILE, THE PHALANGIST FORCES GRADUALLY STARTED ARRIVING.

THEY WERE GOING IN TO PURGE THE CAMPS OF PALESTINIAN TERRORISTS.

AND WE WERE THEIR COVER.

AFTER THAT, WE'D TAKE CONTROL.

ALL NIGHT WE HEARD SHOOTING FROM THE CAMPS, AND THE SKY WAS LIT WITH FLARES.

THE NEXT MORNING THEY STARTED BRINGING OUT THE CIVILIANS.

A LONG ROW OF PEOPLE WAS LED OUT OF THE CAMPS BY THE PHALANGISTS.

FROM OUR HILLTOP, WE SAW A PHALANGIST SOLDIER LEADING AN OLD MAN INTO A BUILDING.

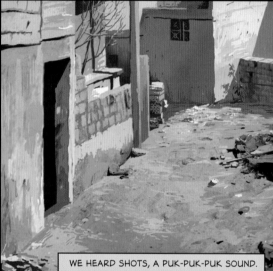

WE HEARD SHOTS, A PUK-PUK-PUK SOUND.

THEN THE SOLDIER CAME OUT ALONE. WE CALLED DOWN TO HIM.

WHAT HAPPENED?

HE STARTED MOTIONING. HE'D TOLD THE MAN TO KNEEL DOWN.	WHEN THE MAN REFUSED, HE SHOT HIM IN THE KNEES...	...THEN IN THE STOMACH, AND FINALLY...	...IN HIS HEAD.

WAS THERE A MOMENT WHEN YOU PUT EVERYTHING TOGETHER, WHEN YOU TOLD YOURSELF: TRUCKS ARE GOING IN EMPTY, COMING OUT PACKED. WOMEN AND CHILDREN ARE LEAVING THE CAMP. THERE'S A BULLDOZER GOING IN. COULD THIS BE A MASSACRE?

YES, OF COURSE. BUT THAT ONLY HAPPENED AT THE POINT WHEN MY MEN SAID, "WE SAW IT."

THEY WERE SITTING ON TOP OF THE TANK.

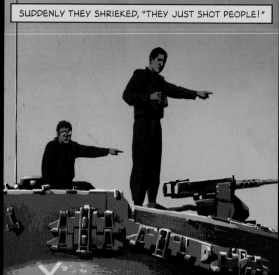

SUDDENLY THEY SHRIEKED, "THEY JUST SHOT PEOPLE!"

MY MEN CLAIMED THEY SAW THE PHALANGISTS STAND PEOPLE UP AGAINST A WALL AND KILL THEM.

THAT'S WHEN I CALLED MY COMMANDING OFFICER DIRECTLY. I TOLD HIM ABOUT ACTIVITIES GOING ON IN THE CAMPS. HE SAID, "WE KNOW, IT'S UNDER CONTROL, WE'VE REPORTED IT." SO AS FAR AS I WAS CONCERNED, THE ISRAELI ARMY KNEW ABOUT IT AND WAS DEALING WITH IT.

THE COMMAND CENTER WAS LOCATED BEHIND US, ABOUT ONE HUNDRED YARDS AWAY, ON TOP OF A VERY TALL BUILDING WHERE THEY COULD LOOK DOWN AND SEE EVERYTHING. THEY PROBABLY HAD A BETTER VIEW THAN I DID.

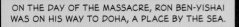

I WAS DRIVING TO THE ARMY'S LANDING FIELD THERE.

ON THE ROADS I NOTICED A LOT OF PHALANGISTS. THEY WERE VERY HAPPY, LIVELY.

I JUST CONTINUED ON MY WAY.

AS SOON AS THEY LEFT, AT 11:30, I KNOCKED BACK HALF A GLASS OF WHISKEY AND CALLED ARIEL SHARON AT HIS RANCH.

HE WAS DROWSY. I SAID, ARIK, I HEAR THE PALESTINIANS ARE BEING MASSACRED BY CHRISTIANS. WE HAVE TO STOP IT.

HE ASKED ME, "DID YOU SEE IT?" I SAID, "NO, BUT THERE ARE PLENTY OF WITNESSES WHO DID." HE SAID, "OKAY. THANK YOU FOR BRINGING IT TO MY ATTENTION."

THERE WAS NOTHING MORE. NOT I'LL CHECK IT OUT, I'LL DO SOMETHING. NOTHING.

HE SAID, "THANK YOU FOR TELLING ME, HAVE A HAPPY NEW YEAR." AND HE WENT TO SLEEP.

ON THE FINAL DAY OF THE MASSACRE, I WAS UP AT ABOUT 5:00 OR 5:30.

I GOT MY TEAM AND DROVE TOWARD SABRA AND SHATILA.

WE ARRIVED THERE AND... WHAT A MESS.

YOU KNOW THE PICTURE OF THE WARSAW GHETTO? THE ONE OF THE BOY WITH HIS HANDS UP? A LONG TRAIN OF WOMEN, OLD PEOPLE, AND CHILDREN WERE WALKING LIKE THAT, WITH THEIR HANDS UP.

THIS WAS THE ACT THAT STOPPED THE MASSACRE. THE PHALANGISTS DISAPPEARED DOWN THE STREET, WHILE THE PALESTINIAN WOMEN AND CHILDREN TURNED BACK TO THE CAMP.

WE WENT IN WITH THEM TO SEE WHAT WAS HAPPENING. INSIDE THE CAMP I SAW A HUGE AMOUNT OF RUBBLE.

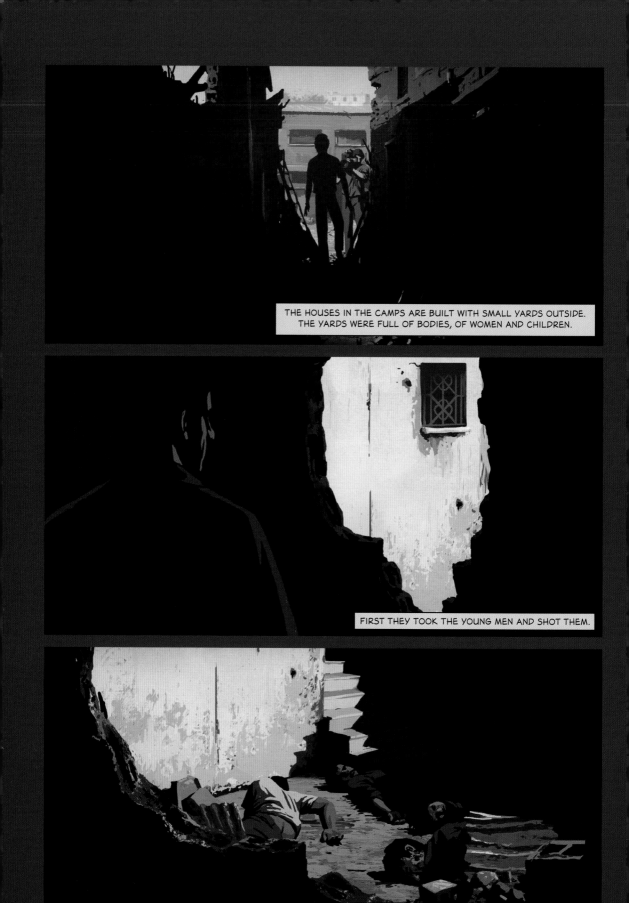

THE HOUSES IN THE CAMPS ARE BUILT WITH SMALL YARDS OUTSIDE. THE YARDS WERE FULL OF BODIES, OF WOMEN AND CHILDREN.

FIRST THEY TOOK THE YOUNG MEN AND SHOT THEM.

THEN THEY SETTLED ACCOUNTS WITH THE FAMILIES.

WE WENT INTO A NARROW ALLEY, ABOUT THE WIDTH OF A MAN AND A HALF. THE ALLEY WAS BLOCKED, TO ABOUT CHEST HEIGHT, WITH THE BODIES OF YOUNG MEN.

AND THEN IT CAME OVER ME: WHAT I WAS LOOKING AT WAS A MASSACRE.

Acknowledgments

This book owes its existence to Riva Hocherman at Metropolitan Books. Her initiative, insight, and patient guidance helped shape every aspect of its creation. Thanks are due to Yoni Goodman, director of animation for the film *Waltz with Bashir,* who developed the movie's storyboards. The illustrations here took their cue from his essential work.   Our thanks as well to Asaf Hanuka, Michael Faust, Tomer Hanuka, and Yaara Buchman, part of the film's illustration team, whose drawings are included in this book. Roi Baron assisted the book's production in ways large and small. Finally, grateful acknowledgment is made to Robin Moyer for use of his photographs of the massacre in the Sabra and Shatila refugee camps.

About the Authors

ARI FOLMAN, a Tel Aviv–based filmmaker, wrote, produced, and directed the animated documentary *Waltz with Bashir*. His previous two feature films, *Saint Clara* and *Made in Israel*, won numerous Israeli academy awards, among them Best Film and Best Director for *Saint Clara*, which also received the People's Choice Award at the 1996 Berlin Film Festival. In addition, Ari Folman produces and writes for television, including for the Israeli series *In Treatment*, which was remade in the United States for HBO.

DAVID POLONSKY was art director and chief illustrator for the animated film *Waltz with Bashir*. His illustrations have appeared in every major Israeli daily and magazine. He has created animated short films for television, received multiple awards for his children's book illustrations, and teaches illustration at Bezalel, Israel's prestigious art academy.